LEADERSHIP

Influential Leadership Skills for Masterful Business Communication, Management Conversations and Team Building

Arthur Cannon

Copyright © Arthur Cannon 2017

All Rights Reserved.

Table of Contents

INTRODUCTION 1

WHAT MAKES A LEADER? 5

    Boss vs Leader 7

    Qualification 8

    Authority, Example and Knowledge 9

    Communication 10

    Dictation, Pace, Pitch, Tone and Volume 12

    Leadership Styles 16

    Self-Development 18

    Someone is always Looking, Someone is always Listening .. 19

    Acuity, Flexibility, Education and Implementation 20

    Charisma and Personal Impact 21

    Increasing your Charisma and Personal Impact 23

SYSTEMATIC THINKING 31

    Learning to Think Systematically 34

    Have a vision 36

    Basic Outcome Clarification Process 37

    On Understanding and Influencing Others 40

    Negotiation Skills 43

    Integrity and Continuity 43

    Rapport 45

    Rapport and Breathing 46

Posture Mirroring 48

Matching Tone and Pace 48

DEVELOPING YOUR TEAM 51

The Seven Stages 52

Giving and Receiving Feedback 56

Group Learning 58

DECISION MAKING 61

MANAGING OUTCOMES 71

Outcomes and Beliefs 71

Directing a Conversation 74

Conflict 76

INFLUENTIAL PHRASES YOU CAN USE TODAY ... 81

QUICK FIRE TACTICS YOU CAN USE TODAY 87

BODY LANGUAGE TIPS 91

BRINGING EVERYTHING TOGETHER 97

Eliminate Zero-Sum Thinking 99

AFTERWORD 101

ABOUT THE AUTHOR 103

INTRODUCTION

Welcome to *Leadership: Influential Leadership Skills for Mastering Business Communication Management Conversations and Team Building*. Instead of page after page of describing the chemical reactions that go on inside our brains when we communicate or age old textbook jargon, this comprehensive book cuts out the filler in order to deliver actionable information that you can start using today. Every page contains relevant information ready to apply and the reader is actively encouraged to add to the information contained and use it to develop their own personal techniques and style. The book was designed to be read cover to cover, however if a certain chapter is of particular interest to you please feel free to jump ahead, for instance skip to the *Influential Phrases* section if you're looking to get a pay rise today.

Each section goes into depth on a different topic. They are arranged as to build upon each other towards the final chapter, which will explain how to put everything together and which leadership styles and methods of communication work best in what situation.

The high level material throughout this book will help you to understand what both superiors and team members require from a leader and how to manage and guide these expectations towards preferential outcomes every time. The book comprises of models, strategies and tactics that reach across various topics and subjects that can either be used individually, or combined to assert your ideas and direct interactions with any number of different people in any given situation. This book is mainly framed inside the working environment but whether you are a football coach, sales manager, financial advisor or entrepreneur this book has information relevant to your day to day business interactions and when used correctly, it will greatly enhance your production and progression within your chosen field.

This book is focused on your experience and should be integrated with what you already know, with the aim of gaining greater influence within your workplace and industry alike. Follow the exercises and decision making models included and you will find an added confidence in both your delegating and management skills.

Understand and learn how to coach the best results out of others through *Systematic Thinking, understanding* and *feedback,* whilst increasing any team's functionality and productivity with the proven outcome management techniques explained within *Managing Outcomes*.

The Chapters *Influential Phrases You can use today* and *Quick Fire Tactics You can use today* were designed to, at a glance provide useful tips and techniques on the most effective ways of asking questions, making requests and delegating.

Your team is your most important resource. Their unique skills and values will contribute to group outcomes in ways

INTRODUCTION

that may often appear random. But through self and team development you will begin to recognise the patterns within the system, sense coming events and know the proper communication and management styles to use in order to successfully influence the situation towards your desired outcome. Do not be at the whim of your surroundings; harness, strengthen and perfect your communication, influence and decision making skills and become the most powerful leader you can be.

WHAT MAKES A LEADER?

A leader doesn't exist as an independent body, it exist as a connection between individuals. An agreement made towards the groups best interests. A leader must be able to recognise where they and their team are and where they are heading and the best way to get there. The best leaders, like mentors, guide us within the frame of developing not only our skillsets but also our individuality.

Leaders have the ability to balance their tremendous creative power with a humble realism. This honesty does not hinder a leader's ability to either think or act, quite the opposite. These attributes lead to a higher quality of action that is congruent with individual and company values and a high level of success.

By setting measurable objectives to use as signposts on the way to achieving a goal the organised leader keeps their team on track. To be an effective leader you will need to master many skills both practical and interpersonal but none more important than the following:

A leader must accept reality and then act accordingly.

Accepting the reality of a situation may not at first appear to be a skill however, being able to disengage from your emotions and preconceptions in order to make the most logical decision does take a lot of practice, you must be vigilant not to let your emotions get the best of you when making decisions.

To act accordingly could mean anything from upgrading your skillset to putting in overtime, it could even mean accepting that a current strategy isn't working and recognising that it is time for change. The key is recognising and accepting the realities and outcomes attached to the current situation and then influencing them to our advantage. This is accomplished through the following traits:

A leader possesses charisma.

A leader has very high levels of influence.

Leaders have outstandingly patience.

Leaders have good attention spans and focus.

A leader is respected by everyone, not just their team.

The best leaders have an ingrained sense of responsibility.

You can spot a leader by the way they are treated by others.

A good leader is confident in being the center of attention and comfortable with not being the center of attention.

Leaders are generally well groomed.

Leaders speak with an air of confidence.

Leaders do not lose their composure.

A leader knows how to do things.

Leaders are constantly looking to improve.

Leaders are inspirational and passionate.

Leaders possess high levels of both transparency and integrity.

Leaders stay calm and composed under pressure.

Leaders are emotionally intelligent.

Extreme flexibility comes with ease to effective leaders.

Leaders talk less and listen more.

Boss vs Leader

Fundamentally the boss vs leader comparison is one of authority vs influence. Below we will further discuss the differences of authority and influence in leadership but now we must consider how we can we tell the difference between a boss and a leader? During your next interaction with a manager/boss/leader pay attention to the following:

A boss uses terms like "I will" or "You will"; a leader says "We will".

A boss demands respect; a leader's manner is one that commands and earns respect.

A boss relies on their position of authority; a leader retains their influence regardless of position.

A leader is gladly followed; a boss is reluctantly obeyed.

A boss uses 'carrots and sticks'; a leader inspires those around them.

Bosses demand time; leaders give time.

Leaders mentor team mates; bosses send subordinates to re-training.

Bosses utilise HR procedures; leaders communicate with individuals.

Leaders have a low staff turnover; bosses are constantly interviewing prospective staff.

A boss is interested in what is wrong; a leader is interested.

A boss holds staff accountable; leaders share responsibility.

Leaders utilise their team's potential; bosses use their staff.

A leader is a role model; bosses inspire fear.

A leader is open to debate; a boss will open the door for you on your way out.

Leaders are responsive; bosses are reactive.

Qualification

Leaders possess many skills and qualifications but it is never the formal qualification that makes the leader. The traits and skills wielded by the most influential of leaders are developed over time with each new skill further advancing the last. The true measure of a leader is the way in which they carry their team through times of change and conflict.

Many team members may contribute to a project but ultimately the decision and responsibility rests with the team leader. This requires that the team leader be able to make appropriate decisions that at times may seem harsh or drastic. The skill to making correct decisions that successfully drive a team forward comes with experience, however there are useful decision making models contained within this book that will act as stabilisers whilst experience is built.

Authority, Example and Knowledge

Authority and leadership are not synonymous. In many cases the authority of the leader is something that is only perceived from the outside of the group dynamic. A leader's authority can be better described as their influence and the level of a leader's influence can be measured by the quality of the relationships they have with their followers. Therefor individuals with positions of authority can only be deemed leaders if they can successfully influence others. Within successful teams the leader is often viewed as a comrade as oppose to a superior. At times of change a leader takes control and pulls their team through, where an authority figure would push their team forcing them through. In conclusion, the influence of a masterful leader is far superior to the threats of an authority figure.

True leaders lead by **Example** they lead from the front taking responsibility for both themselves and their team. A leader should have the experience and knowledge to be able to move ahead of their team guiding them towards desired outcomes and through any difficult times. Be sure your actions are congruent with the things you say, avoid saying one thing and doing another at all costs as this will have a negative impact on your perceived authenticity.

Knowledge used to be power, not anymore. We live in an age where knowledge is cheap and therefore under-valued and underused. Thanks to the internet we have access to practically limitless information; the key is how we apply that information. Power in the modern age is creativity. The way we use and implement our knowledge is the true measure of our intelligence as individuals. We can change the world through rational observation (derived from knowledge and experience) and creativity, which are the cornerstones of both influence and innovation. When we lack knowledge we severely limit our creative capabilities, our options, influence and our chances of success.

Communication

Communication skills on some level are essential for success in any field. These skills allow us to better understand and cooperate with those around us. In business or when we are managing a team, clear communication is especially crucial as communication skills will greatly effect negotiations in your favour. Within working environments good communications build trust and reliability as well as lowering mistakes and boosting productivity. Workplace communication has been proven to increase staff moral and responsibility, especially if staff and team members have the ability to communicate both horizontally across and vertically up the chain of command. There are also many monetary benefits to sharpening your communication skills that are not at first obvious. Promotion and affiliate marketing for a start, but that will be covered in another book later in the series.

Advanced communication skills will enhance your leadership quality, sphere of influence and chances of success for the rest of your life. The best communicators are also masters of nonverbal communication skills such as body language. Before we go any further here's a quick tip. Decide on the tone of the message you are trying to convey before you begin. This will help you to stay detached from emotional triggers and allow for greater acuity. Examples:

Friendly

Clear and Concise (straight to the point)

Empathetic

Apologetic

Forgiving

Confidence

Respectful

Cautious

Guiding/Advice

Praise

Dictation, Pace, Pitch, Tone and Volume

A great deal of the information we communicate we convey through what we say. But do not be fooled into thinking it is the words we choose that transfer the information that our message conveys. Audiences receive the most information from the way in which we speak, not from the words we use. Our dictation gives a way a lot of personal information as will our pace. Tone, pitch and volume transmit a great deal about our current feeling towards whatever is being discussed. We all have a natural inbuilt ability to 'read' others via their pace, pitch tone and volume, dictation is more of a nurtured learning.

Dictation, along with good enunciation and clear pronunciation will make things much easier for your audience, allowing them to focus on your message. Practice simplifying sentences by eliminating unnecessary words in order to ensure you are as understandable as possible.

Work on the proper stresses of words, this helps to convey emotion and really brings your point home.

Pace or speaking rate is most commonly measured in words per minute but at times can be measured in syllables per minute. This of course varies from language to language but for today we'll stick to English and an average word count per minute. Analysis of professional speakers shows us that ideally we want to be using between 150 and 180 words per minute depending on the situation. Varying your speaking rate throughout your conversation, presentation or pitch will help to increase and maintain audience attention and therefor add to your perceived charisma. When on the road to mastering speaking rate, be sure to pay attention to the complexity of the content and the clarity of both your language and vision.

Pitch is something we generally have good control over, however to get a full sound from your vocal chords it is important that they stay hydrated. Further to hydration, before public speaking (every morning before leaving the house!) try humming for a few minutes, varying both pitch and tone. This exercise will warm up your voice allowing for greater range when speaking in public.

A friendly **Tone** of voice is reassuring; it lets you know you can trust the person you are speaking to and that they can be relied upon. To develop a friendly tone you must first decide what tones sound friendly to you and begin to mirror the types of tones that suit your tone and accent. If you have a strong accent, eliminate the regional slang from your vocabulary in order to become more understandable.

When speaking from the heart a relaxed pace and slightly deeper than usual tone will convey the depth of your message.

If you're speaking, ideally you'll want to be heard. If you need to increase your **Volume** do not shout, this will only stress your vocal chords and your voice will sound strained. If you require greater volume, speak firmly from your diaphragm by tensing your stomach and lower back muscles as this will add further depth to your voice, carrying it further without sacrificing the quality of your tone of voice or your message.

Face your audience

Some people develop the habit of not looking directly at their audience, they may look at the floor, a light or an empty seat, but this in itself demonstrates a lack in confidence and a lower value. Not looking directly at the audience may help with confidence issues; however those who choose this method miss out on one of the voices natural applications. When we are looking at another person our voices automatically modulate in order for the individual to be able to hear us when we speak. Use this natural talent to your advantage.

Humming

Warming up your voice is not only for singers, each morning and before any public presentation the voice should be prepared for action. Start with a low, deep pitch paying attention the vibrations within your chest. After a few seconds of low humming raise the pitch slightly and continue to do so every five seconds.

Tongue Twisters

Tongue twisters are an ideal way of sharpening not just our elocution; they also help us to sharpen our memory skills and gain in confidence.

Food and drink

It is a given that we must drink plenty of water in order to stay hydrated. Beyond water try mixing in some lemon and honey to soothe vocal chords, herbal tea works great too.

Avoid throat irritants like fizzy drinks, alcohol, energy drinks, fruit juices and anything containing caffeine. Dairy products also have an adverse effect on our voices by causing excess phlegm to develop.

Spicy foods are particularly good at loosening the phlegm that naturally forms in our throat and can at times cause a voice to sound raspy or forced.

This one should go without saying however it does bear mentioning that smoking inflicts serious damage to our throats and vocal chords and quitting should be seriously considered. Smoking is not a habit of the rational.

Leadership Styles

There are as many different leadership styles out there as there are leaders struggling to adopt them. Entire libraries exist dedicated to implementing the numerous management techniques available, but the fact remains that each person is different and must adopt a style that works for them and their goals. Becoming a true leader ultimately means developing your own style and strategies that leverage on your own practical and interpersonal skills. However, below I have explained some of the more successful styles currently in use to give you some basic ideas.

Autocratic Leadership is a leadership style where the focus is on the leader. All decisions are reached by the leader alone without consulting subordinates and then tasks are passed down through the ranks. Autocratic leaders are often forced to rely on formal policies, processes and procedures to help them manage without the direct input of their team. Autocratic leaders are not usually the most popular bosses and the style brings inherent issues, however it does work for some people, there are some extremely powerful autocratic leaders out there.

Managers and leaders who utilise the **Democratic Leadership** style rely on the input of others before taking action. Team members and subordinates are valued in the decision making process, however the responsibility remains with the leader or manager who has had the final say on matters such as delegation, targets and timescales.

Adopters of the **Charismatic leadership** style are visionaries who value individuality. They recognise that each person has different skills to offer. The charismatic leader directs their team as to actualise their vision through personal impact, respect and the power of their personality. People naturally gravitate towards charismatic leaders; they inspire those around them in to action and are great to work with.

The **Coaching leadership** style is becoming more widespread and popular. The coaching leader or mentor closely supervises their team and develops each member's skills in order to optimise each individual and therefore improve results of the team as a whole. This is an extremely productive environment that creates valuable and loyal individuals.

The **Facilitative Leadership** style requires a high level of acuity to master. Facilitative leaders delicately direct their team depending on their current results. If a team is failing or becoming complacent the facilitative leader will adopt a more hands on approach, managing each task step by step if required. When managing a high functioning team, the facilitative leader will take more of a background position allowing the team to continue to successfully operate through their own initiative.

Strategic Leaders focus on the organisation as a whole instead of the usual top to bottom approach. Effective strategic leaders are able to produce the expected standard of results even in times of great change, without disruption. An expert in the strategic leadership style will operate on all levels of a business (usually behind the scenes), linking people and departments, successfully facilitating the flow of information and production throughout a company. Strategic leaders are high functioning individuals who are prone to success.

Transactional leadership is as it sounds. If the group or individual completes their allotted task or reaches pre-agreed targets, they are rewarded (usually by commission). It may seem pretty basic but this style has its benefits. A team that operates within transactional leadership will generally have clear guidelines, allowing each team member to know where they stand and what is expected of them. This is a sink or swim environment which is focused on expectations, where the rewards are great but the employee drop off rate and stress is high.

Self-Development

The best leaders are on a constant path of self-development and discovery, the skills from which are then used to develop others around them. The cornerstone of self-development is to recognise your own thoughts and actions as well as the consequences involved. Over time you will begin to notice your behavioural patterns, at which point you can begin to modify and change them. The first thing to remember is:

Your thoughts become words.

Your words determine your actions.

Your actions become your habits.

Your habits determine your character.

Your thoughts are not your beliefs; they only reflect your beliefs and rarely are they entirely accurate. The main thing about beliefs is that they work in one of two ways, they either enable you or they limit you. Pay close attention to your beliefs and the impact they have on your day to day life, take a mental note whether the belief is limiting or enabling your potential success.

Someone is always Looking, Someone is always Listening

Someone is always looking, someone is always listening and so you must always present yourself in the best possible light. We expect it during job interviews and dinners with the in-laws, however in these modern times more than ever we are in the spotlight and therefore must be aware of the perceptions of others. The perceptions of others are not to be feared. With a little self-awareness we can ensure that we make great first impressions that last, and with continuity and integrity of character we will always project a positive self. In order to prepare for an interaction try asking yourself a few basic questions, the questions below will help you in not making errors of judgement when presenting yourself.

Where am I going?

Who will be there?

What is expected of me?

What is the excepted dress code?

What will I say to whom?

What are my objectives?

Acuity, Flexibility, Education and Implementation

Acuity is an enhanced awareness of yourself, your actions, your surroundings and the results you achieve. Acuity and awareness are extremely valuable skills to develop which will enable you to find out if what you are doing is getting you what you want. After analysing your own actions and their outcomes, you now have options to consider. Typically whoever has the most options (due to their flexibility) will have the most influence in any given situation. Once you have looked at your current outcomes you may need to adjust and redirected yourself slightly in order to better define your outcomes, this may require that you learn a new skill or even just a change in perspective. You have now recognised the results and the adjustments required to improve them, all that is left is to internalise your new skills or methods and apply them in the correct manner.

Wash, rinse and repeat the above method on a regular basis and you will stay current with your skillset as well as gaining a habit of self-improvement and personal development. As you properly direct and re-direct your actions through the analysis of your results you will find your results to be of a much higher quality and your goals much quicker to reach.

The effect of this habitual improvement will drive a team forward through development of the individual, creating confident and competent team members with an imbedded culture of excellence. This is one of the ways in which a leader maintains the enduring respect required to manage a team long term.

Charisma and Personal Impact

Personal impact can be described as charisma, but charisma is difficult to measure however its power rises above social standing, wealth and destroys preconceived prejudices. Mysterious in nature, charisma is thought to be the gift of the chosen few and a very powerful gift at that. In reality charisma is the ability to make an outstanding, emotionally charged and lasting impression on those we meet. Those who have and utilise their charisma naturally influence those around them as they radiate both competence and confidence.

When it comes down to it, charisma and likability are elusive concepts to grasp. But what it comes down to is how others feel when they are around you. We can focus on the traits of enigmatic communicators and leaders from the past and see what they have to teach us. My experience within the sales industry led me to discover actionable methods of increasing my impact within any interaction. As mentioned earlier, the first steps are self-awareness and flexibility followed by education and implementation. With the aim of gaining greater personal impact, the areas you will focus on will be localised, working on the individual areas, and leveraging them against one another will greatly enhance your perceived charisma and the personal impact you make on the people you meet (an example of leveraging is that a proper posture will greatly improve your speaking voice).

Indicators that you need to work on your charisma and personal impact:

- I suffer from anxiety especially when giving presentations.
- I am an introvert.
- I often find myself looking at the ground.

- I often feel defensive.
- Sometimes I find it hard to express how I feel.
- People tell me I mumble.
- My posture isn't the best/I often 'hunch' my back.
- My ideas often get ignored or rejected.
- I am hesitant.
- I sometimes struggle with decisions.
- Whenever I speak I seem to get the reaction "yeah, but".
- People often misread my intentions.
- I get nervous when 'opening' new clients or speaking to new people.
- I get on well with clients but struggle to 'close'.
- I regularly use filler words like "um" and "uh".

Increasing your Charisma and Personal Impact

There are many ways to increase your perceived charisma and personal impact but here I will only be discussing methods that call for no investment and can be implemented today. We all develop bad habits over time, and we need to keep ourselves in check to guarantee that we are making the most of ourselves and our situation. A lot of your charisma comes down to your resourcefulness;

you must use what you have effectively and without self-doubt.

Breathing

When speaking, try to breathe slowly and deeply projecting from your lower lungs. This will allow for a fuller sounding, more confident tone and greater volume control.

Proper fitting clothes

Do not underestimate the effect of proper fitting clothes, I know this seems obvious but we all know people who dress in what they feel is fashionable but other people feel is inappropriate. Do not do this! In formal or working environments, conservative and appropriately fitting outfits must be worn. A well-fitting suit goes a long way.

Posture

Your posture affects many aspects besides how others will perceive you. A good and proper posture will allow for more effective work with less fatigue caused to the body as well as greatly enhancing the voice. Keep an eye on your posture, bad habits are easily developed. Correct those slouches and sit up straight!

Voice

Your voice is the easiest way to project confidence and charisma, the voice is the most pliable tool available to you and should be treated as such. It would be a good idea to listen to famous speakers such as Anthony Robbins and pay special attention to stand-up comics to gain insights on delivery. Here are some tips you can try out right now to improve the quality of your speaking voice:

Whilst speaking try tensing your abs, this will help to project your voice from the diaphragm.

You may tense your abs and lower back to enhance your voice but the rest of your body should be as relaxed as possible.

If standing, position your feet with one slightly in front of the other with your weight shifted slightly forward.

Position your shoulders back and slide them down in order to straighten your back and lift your head, with your chin parallel to the ground neither lowered of lifted.

Working on Posture? Take a Good Look in the Mirror

Ok well, maybe not a mirror but take 2 full length photos of yourself, one front on and one from the side. Once you have your photos, cross reference them with the list below to diagnose and fix any posture problems.

- Is your ear positioned in front of the midpoint of your shoulder? If yes, your head is orientated too far forward.

- If your shoulder blade is visible, that means your back is too curved.

- If your hips push forward, this arches your lower spine significantly. This condition is diagnosed as an anterior pelvic tilt.

- Look at your shoulders. Does one appear higher than the other? It shouldn't.

- Do your kneecaps point inward?

- Do your toes point inward or outward more than 10 degrees?

If you suffer from rounded shoulders, complete the following:

Lie face down on the floor, with each arm at a 90° angle with your palms face down. Without changing your elbow angle, raise both arms by pulling your shoulders back and hold for five seconds. Complete 3 sets of 15 repetitions daily.

Poor head movement due to stiff neck:

Moving only your head, lower your chin toward your chest in order to stretch out the back of your neck. Hold for five seconds and repeat at least 10 times daily.

Misaligned or elevated shoulders:

Sit up straight in a chair with your hands by your sides, arms straight, palms face down on the seat. Now, without moving your arms, push down on the chair until your hips lift up off the seat and your torso rises. Hold this for five seconds. Complete 3 sets of 15 repetitions daily.

Presence

The transformative power of presence is often the most desired trait associated with charisma. Social standing and influence is often assessed by the quality and strength of your presence. Being present in the moment adds massively to the quality and depth of your presence but what is meant by being present? Our minds naturally shift their orientation and thinking styles on a moment by moment basis, these mental shifts can be triggered by practically anything. In order to stay present we must be aware of our mental states and get rid of any bad habits that we have picked up along the way. Throughout life we all develop habits that have a negative effect on our perceived presence such as selfishness, boasting, temper tantrums, tardiness, and general unreliability. We must keep a close eye out for these negative traits and eradicate them upon discovery. Our emotions are our best tool in reading our internal state, but how do we read our own emotions? And how does this affect our presence? How we are feeling is in effect a gauge of how we are thinking and how we are thinking dictates our level of presence in the current moment. In order to 'be' in the present moment our thinking must be focused on the present and not on the past or future. Here's how emotions and timelines coincide with your current state and being present:

Anger is a reactionary emotion caused by thinking about the past.

Sadness too indicates we are thinking about the past (anger can be recognised as the bodyguard of sad).

Fear and worry arise when we are thinking about future events.

Happy/calm and the feeling of time 'flying' is a clear indication that you are present in the moment.

In summary, if we wish to be in the present moment our thinking must be focused on the present and not in the past or future. Once we are fully present we are able to focus on and improve the overall impact of our presence, which can be increased by:

Making meaningful eye contact with every person present when entering a room, accompanied by a warm smile.

Letting others speak first, don't be in a rush to speak. A moments silence will allow all parties to adjust to your presence. If your audience is restless allow them to settle before you begin.

Become present by first closing your eyes, take a deep breath and hold it for five seconds. Noticing how the wind feels on your skin, focus your attention of different body parts, left arm, left leg, right leg and finally right arm. This will return your attention to the present.

Those with presence radiate energy, but where does this energy come from? Within us we have two primary energetic forces which we can harness to increase our actual and perceived energy levels. Firstly we draw energy from our psychical selves, the alertness and readiness of our entire bodies, do not lose this source of energy to nervousness and self-doubt. Secondly we draw energy from our individual selves, by that we mean our experience and personalities. When our actions are congruent with our values and feelings our actions are exponentially energised by our individual selves. If we find ourselves lacking in motivation we must realign our values and the situation or task at hand. In instances where our values cannot be aligned with, or are in direct opposition to our proposed task or course of action the proposed task should be redefined or rejected.

SYSTEMATIC THINKING

The way we do what we do to achieve our outcomes is a step beyond standard strategizing and so will be referred to as systematic thinking. An essential aspect of systematic thinking comes from recognising the internal representations of both ourselves and others. We should all be aware of how our internal representations and mind-set correspond to our external behaviours and resulting outcomes.

Effective systematic thinking arises by combining a working set of critical thinking skills. By using strategic processes systematic thinkers are able to successfully predict, evaluate and influence coming events. In order to give our systematic thinking skills a boost, we must first discern and understand the separate aspects involved and focus on each, before finally putting everything back together in a way that suits our individual styles, values and goals. To be able to recognise the connections between your internal state, representations and external behaviours you should ask yourself the following questions:

What is my current state?

What are my first impressions of the matter at hand?

How do the individual components of the issue relate to me?

How have my behaviours affected the process?

How has the process affected my behaviours?

In what way do I plan to influence the system/situation?

Is the current process actually failing? In many cases processes work exceedingly well, just not in the way we first anticipated.

Are my internal representations and state a root cause of any trouble?

Is the current situation or trouble the root cause of my internal state?

What is the value of this situation?

Has this issue or similar issues been dealt with in the past?

If so how was it dealt with?

Our brain has two halves, the left hemisphere and the right hemisphere. Each of these hemispheres is thought to control opposing mental faculties. Our left hemispheres are in charge of our rational and logical thinking; whilst creativity is locate within the right hemisphere. Each of us naturally favours a particular style of thinking; some of us are creatives and favour the right side whilst some favour a more left sided and formal approach. An important aspect of systematic thinking is the ability to utilise both the left and right sides of the brain, rapidly shifting from divergent to convergent thinking to effectively navigate a situation.

There are a number of methods that can help us to sharpen our ability.

New Stimulations

Whenever we get out of our comfort zones or try new things our rational and creative minds naturally work together. New situations awaken our creative mind whilst simultaneously using our logical thinking to assess risks and opportunities. All this happens extremely quickly and naturally. Exposing yourself to new and challenging situations is a great way of forcing your mind to think in new ways and can also be a lot of fun.

Pay Attention to the Newest Ideas

Inspiration can come from anywhere at any time, pay attention to and collect the newest ideas. Fresh concepts fuel change so encourage your team to keep one eye on innovation and together you will stay ahead of the curve.

Increase your knowledge

Experience alone is not enough to become expert problem solvers. Knowledge increases our potential for devising outcomes. A sound knowledge base and inventive attitude are the most valuable of attributes.

Interact with as many People as Possible (without wasting your time)

Exchanging ideas with peers is exciting, a creative bubble surrounds those involved and innovation is assured. Interacting with people from other industries can lead to new insights, massive change and networking opportunities.

Take up Challenging Tasks and Puzzles as a Pastime

Mastering a new language or musical instrument is fantastic for making simultaneous use of both hemispheres of the brain. Puzzles and brainteasers also encourage us to think in both logical and creative ways.

Take Time Out

It's important that everyone on your team takes rest and relaxation on a regular basis. Actively encourage your team to take time out, often when people return from short breaks they are full of ideas and positivity.

Learning to Think Systematically

Fundamentally understanding systematic thinking should not be thought of as an understanding of systems. It is an understanding of how the daily problems we all face come about.

Difficulties in problem solving often arise from failure to realise that **incidents are not isolated**, they occur in relation to each other.

SYSTEMATIC THINKING

Complex issues can only be solved with systematic thinking. 'Winging it' will only lead to unintended consequences, potentially making the issue worse.

Patterns occur constantly. If we consider our lives a story, these regular patterns would be represented by reoccurring story arcs with similar themes. These archetypal themes should be viewed as a sign of either coming or required behavioural change.

Look for **points of leverage.** Achieving optimal results often means acting within a process or system, from a point that may at first seem counterintuitive.

Recognise that most **problems are best addressed through multiple methods** and solutions working in concert. Ignore the tendency of believe a problem can be polarized around a single solution.

View the entire system as a family. Family members even though related in fact have their own lives and agendas. Family member's actions may at times provide unexpected results even though as a group they are extremely close nit. The level of complexity of the interactions within a system, family or team is such that they will regularly cause results that nobody wants.

Make a deep commitment to learning to **develop the courage to be wrong**. Mastery comes from analysing our own mental models and processes.

Develop a **long term vs short term** way of thinking, learning along the way to give up short term gratification for long term investment in success.

Systematic thinking does not allow for opportunistic thinking which is often a risky and emotional decision. That does not mean systematic thinkers are not opportunists, it simply means that even opportunities must be properly evaluated.

We spend much time focusing on the intelligence of individuals (this is in fact the problem with education today). **Collective or social smarts** are not about the smartest guy in the room. A team should revolve around collective smarts and what we can accomplish as a collective.

Have a vision

Your vision is generally a clear picture of where you want to be, but the path to making this vision a reality is littered with smaller goals and challenges to overcome. Each goal should represent a benchmark along your path and these goals should each be broken down into manageable objectives that can be completed within a deadline.

To have a vision may sound a little philosophical but in essence when communicating your ideas to others your vision only requires two aspects. When presenting your vision in a professional environment, it should be handled similarly to a sales pitch, however in this case the audience is made of superiors and/or teammates and what you want them to buy is your idea and not products or services. Your vision must motivate you and it must also have the ability to inspire others into action. As your vision is described it will create an image of the future, a future that's better for everyone and everyone will make it there together by following your leadership.

As well as the two main aspects mentioned above, when communicating your vision to others you'll want it to include answers to the following:

What will you/your team achieve?

Does the vision have congruent values?

How will it affect you/your team long term?

How long will it take?

What do you need to achieve your vision?

Exactly what will it take to succeed?

How will success be measured?

Will this success cause anyone else's failure?

Does this vision contain long term or short term solutions?

Basic Outcome Clarification Process

Every situation is different and not all rules can be applied to all circumstances but generally speaking the feasibility of your task should be put through a process to clarify the costs, benefits and overall feasibility of any given project or task. There are some basic considerations that need attention prior to sharing your vision. It's always worth remembering that in business it's always best to 'follow the green not the dream', meaning do what is profitable, be flexible with your dreams.

How will the outcome affect those around me?

Be ethical, no one wants to have a negative effect on those around them. In most cases you will find that what's best for the team is also best for the individual. I would strongly advise against sacrificing others for anything other than saving the business or team as a whole. Never risk the safety and wellbeing of others for financial gain.

Will the outcome be an asset, expense or liability?

This is a very important question and many ideas will not pass this stage. This is not a book about financial education, however it is very important to categorise any project by its outcomes in the following ways:

An **asset** will provide for you 'long term' by adding to your cash flow on a regular basis or by boosting the value of existing assets. Not all assets are financial, an asset can be anything that continually adds to or strengthens your business or team.

An **expense** can generally be classed alongside essential running costs and one off payments. Be sure your expenses are not liabilities in disguise. Once you are clear that your expense is in fact an expense you must take a second thought to consider is it worth it? (Whatever it may be).

Avoid **liabilities**. Liabilities cost you on a daily, weekly or monthly basis with little to no gain. A common mistake people make is assuming a car is an asset, when in fact for some individuals a car is clearly a liability that runs above their means. Some people take this example to the extreme and purchase cars on finance, assuring a constant flow of cash will be leaving their accounts for the foreseeable future.

Benefits and Costs

When assessing the benefits of an outcome we must again utilise our acuity. The proper assessment of benefits vs cost will involve a number of factors that all affect each other.

Financial

Short term costs vs short term benefits. Long term costs vs long term benefits. Short term costs vs long term benefits.

Long term costs for short term benefits should not even be considered.

Timescale

Firstly, is the timescale under my control? Will perusing this outcome delay other projects?

Current processes

Any actions undertaken or updates made to processes should preserve the benefits of your current actions. Sacrificing efficiency in one area to improve another will cause you to 'double back' at a later date. If the solution to one problem causes another, this means your solution is faulty. You should return to the brainstorming stage.

Be Smarterr

Make a mental note of the acronym, **SMARTERR** that can help us remember the fundamentals of outcome clarification. Is your outcome **Specific, Measurable, Attainable** and **Rational** with a **Timescale**. Once an outcome is reached it must be **Evaluated** and **Refined** and finally its success should be **Repeated**.

On Understanding and Influencing Others

Have you ever wondered how two individuals can have the same conversation and each come away with different ideas about what was discussed. At times we experience events with others only to later argue about what actually happened. How is this possible? Throughout the day we are bombarded with a constant flow of information and our brains are limited in the amount of information it can take can observe and process at any one time. The way we select information is largely unconscious and loosely based around our favoured sense. For example, where one individual may remember more of what they saw another individual may remember more of what was said. From what is remembered, meaning is created by the individual experiencing the events. Each of us processes information in our own unique way and it's important that we understand this if we wish to successfully understand others.

The vast majority of the information we come across during the day is lost or discounted along the way, much of what we are left with is the information we use to make decisions. Once gathered, the information we collect during the day is then filtered through our personal interpretations: political, cultural, social, inner meanings and assumptions. These interpretations fuel our thought processes which in turn affects our emotional states.

To understand others we must learn to reverse engineer their actions and emotions in order to discern their thought process which leads to their personal interpretation of the events and intentions. By looking into other's actions in this way we can develop a deeper understanding of the individual's personal beliefs and thought processes.

Communicating to an individual's beliefs is not just an influential technique. The benefits are at least threefold:

Deeper understanding creates more meaningful relationships and trust.

You lower the risk of misinterpretation.

A belief is likely to inspire someone to action.

In Business

Understanding an organisation is very similar to understanding an individual. It is common place now for a company to have a written list of values (usually consisting of buzz words). From these values we can perceive the way the organisation sees itself and wishes to be seen by others.

There are two subliminal questions that any company or individual always asks themselves when deciding whether or not to do business with any given organisation:

Do I feel like this is a good deal?

Do I like the company/individual I am dealing with?

It is your goal to answer both of these questions in the affirmative before they arise. To do this there are a number of strategies and tactics available to you, some of which work best face to face and some are better suited to telephone conversations or email.

Negotiation Skills

A negotiation can be defined as any interaction where two or more parties follow pre-agreed guidelines in order to foster mutually beneficial situations. There are rules to follow during negotiations, without which would soon descend into madness. The following will greatly increase your chances of success during negotiations.

Prior to any negotiating, position yourself at an angle from your counterpart as not to sit directly opposite them.

Be clear about what is important.

Discuss the negotiation as if it is a shared problem.

During negotiations be sure to move towards goals, as appose to moving away from problems.

If someone makes you an offer, discuss the offer in full before continuing or considering your counter offer.

When negotiating use forthright questioning as oppose to statements.

At the end of the negotiation process summarise all of the points covered and any progress made. This will ensure there are no misinterpretations.

Integrity and Continuity

As individuals, our characters and authenticity are measured largely by our integrity, or our perceived integrity. Honouring commitments makes us honest, reliable and ultimately, happy. Integrity is one of the most valuable traits an individual can develop alongside intelligence, persistence and determination. At times your integrity will be tried and tested; these moments often turn out to be character defining moments and should not be taken lightly.

Honesty and integrity within a team will produce consistent results of the highest quality. Trust within a team is massively important; you must lead your team with integrity. Being true to your word is never more important than when your team is facing times of change. Team leaders and managers alike may at time want to restrict the flow of information to their team in order to protect them, but this strategy will backfire every time and your team will lose faith in both your integrity and leadership abilities.

In the business world continuity leads to sustainability therefore integrity can be viewed as central to an effective strategy. Cleverly devised business plans are clearly aligned with business policies and organisational structures at conception and the varying factors are assessed in order of importance. Once established, sustaining organisational continuity and integrity are essential if a business is to successfully navigate the pitfalls of the business world. An ethical organisation's due diligence and planning will go beyond the standard compliance issues and health & safety because it is both ethically morally correct to do so.

To maintain organisational integrity, a business must adopt a mixed approach of both formal and informal models and processes that reach legal standards as well as upholding company values. These values and processes must be clear, simple and embody the general collective moral framework of the employees.

Remember: It is always better to turn a task down than agree to something that you cannot deliver on time or in full. Beyond just keeping your word, being able to deliver has an effect on those around you. For example; if you were to plan an event and 24 hours before you found out that there would be a low level of attendance, it would ultimately still be in your best interests to go ahead with the event. It would mean a lot to the people who do attend and your integrity and continuity would still be intact.

Rapport

To have rapport with a person or group is to have a harmonious understanding of ideas and feelings and a natural flow of communication between the individuals involved. Developing your rapport skills should be considered essential learning for anyone who wishes to succeed in the business world. The mutual trust and respect gained through good rapport leads to meaningful and lasting relationships. Being able to communicate effectively is a highly prized skill and once established, a good rapport will support you throughout your personal and business relationships. There are many schools of thought dedicated to gaining and maintaining rapport from NLP (Neuro Linguistic Programming) and block psychological techniques to marketing and advertising and even your bog standard cold calling scripts.

How do we gain and maintain rapport? There are many things to consider before you attempt to increase the current levels of rapport. Attempting to use methods and techniques to build rapport can be very risky and when not done properly can easily be seen through, meaning that the interaction will come across as contrived. This will have the opposite of the desired effect and levels of rapport will significantly drop. You must be both confident and competent if you wish to apply learnt skills to natural interactions; the best interactions have an air of natural spontaneity about them and easily flow towards mutually beneficial conclusions. If your communication style lacks rapport you will be deemed boring, predictable and maybe even rude. Below are some tried and tested techniques for building rapport.

Rapport and Breathing

Pay attention to the breathing patterns of the people you are interacting with, how do they breathe? Deep or shallow breaths? Long or short? How does their breathing pattern affect the pauses in speech? Breathing patterns can be viewed as the underlying rhythm of the interaction.

Below there are some generalised meanings that can be gleaned through monitoring an individual's breathing patterns. It is important to remember that these rules do not apply in every situation. Each person has their own individual communication style, aspects such as medical conditions and bad habits can make successfully reading an individual more of a fluid process rather than a rigid guideline.

Shallow breathing may indicate that an individual is feeling nervous or uneasy.

Fast breathing indicates fear, high stress or anger.

A fast deep breath or forced sigh indicates increasing stress.

Slow deep breaths usually indicate relaxation or concentration.

Once you have locked onto to someone's breathing pattern, gradually modulate your breathing to match theirs and continue as normal. Take note of the effect this has on the interaction. Mirroring (copying/mimicking) an individual's breathing pattern has another valuable benefit, when applied correctly someone can be lead into a different state. Once in sync with someone's breathing pattern you will be able to gently increase or decrease your own breathing pattern, the person you are interacting with you follow your lead and increase or decrease their own breathing rate, therefore being led to either calm down or become energised.

Posture Mirroring

Beware of posture mirroring; it is very easy to spot when done incorrectly. If you are caught out copying someone's posture you will feel pretty foolish. Start by paying more attention to people's postures in general and you will begin to notice people matching each other's postures everywhere.

Copying someone's exact movements and posture is not necessary. The mirroring effect can be achieved with something as slight as a hand movement. A good place to start is to practice naturally taking a sip from your drink at the same time as those you are with.

Matching Tone and Pace

Tone of voice is rarely used to full effect but in reality a great deal of information is portrayed through our tone, even more so than the words we choose to communicate with.

A fast pace and high tone indicates the speaker is tense, nervous or even scared.

A neutral tone and slow pace indicates boredom or sadness.

A loud, erratic tone and pace indicates excitement and/or anger.

A low volume and tone indicates insecurities.

A rhythmic pace and light tone indicates happiness.

A steady pace and proper use of varying tone indicates confidence and competence.

When communicating with someone pay special attention to their tone of voice and try to discern their current underlying mood. Once you have an idea of their emotional state, choose a desired state. Then with subtly, closely match their tone and pace, follow on to slowly change your tone and pace in order to lead them to a new positive state.

The methods and techniques mentioned above should be practiced individually one at a time until each one is second nature. At first these skills will not come naturally but through practice you will internalise them and be able apply them singularly or combined in any way that suits the situation.

DEVELOPING YOUR TEAM

Your team is your most important resource. Their unique skills and values will contribute to group outcomes in ways that may often appear random. But through self and team development you will begin to recognise the patterns within the system, sense coming events and know the proper communication and management styles to use in order to successfully influence the situation towards your desired outcome.

Your team are highly valuable assets and by investing your time and understanding into them, both individually and as a whole you will not only see yourself grow as a leader but also maximise your team's potential. By leveraging your team's individual skills against each other in the correct way, you can optimize your entire process. For instance, in a cold calling sales environment you may have an experienced "opener" calling clients and introducing them to the company, who will then transfer the client to a "closer" who then closes the sale.

Don't get irritated or too pushy, this will annoy everyone every time. You may very well be right but as with Newton's Law of reciprocal action (any action will have an equal and opposite reaction), if you push you get pushed back, by team members, superiors and clients alike.

To successfully manage your team's individual and group development you must be aware of how each person fits in, what they offer and how best to utilise them. Prior to starting any group task, a leader should ask themselves the following questions:

Can we accomplish this task?

What resources do we require to complete the task?

What resources do we already have?

What are our strengths in this field?

What are our weaknesses?

As a leader, what leadership style should I employ to best complete this task?

Remember: Develop, adapt and apply.

Remember: As a leader, you know you are working well when no one realises you even exist.

The Seven Stages

There are seven main stages a team will go through on the journey to completing a goal or group task. We may try to shorten this process and miss stages out but experience will teach those that do that any stage missed will need to be returned to later on. Each of the seven stages raises its own issues; these are handled by keeping an open line of communication and feedback between the entire team. Each stage dictates that a leader asks their team certain questions in order to measure progress. It is a leader's responsibility to lead their team through the seven stages by taking the first step; this leaves a leader vulnerable to making errors. Ensure these errors do not become mistakes by addressing them at the time.

The first stage of any project is **Orientation**. At this point a leader outlines the current situation, how we got here, team identity, purpose and values. The orientation stage is important as it lays out the overall direction and requirements of the team.

The second stage, **Conception or Brainstorming** calls upon the forthrightness of the team as a whole. A team that works from a foundation of mutual regard will bring countless insights to the table. If the brainstorming phase is disregarded then the team will be uncertain and disorientated or worse, fearful and untrusting.

When **Outlining Objectives** and clarifying goals, the aim is to clearly establish what is required by whom, their integrated goals and the vision the team shares as a whole. If the individual roles and goals are not clarified with the rest of the team this could cause people to be sceptical of the task as a whole, meaning that at a later date this stage must be returned to for a thorough explanation.

The **Commitment** phase is the final stage in the development of the task at hand. Now everyone has clear and measurable goals, decisions have been made and now the team is ready to act. If left unresolved the commitment phase will backfire completely causing some team members to resist the plan as a whole. Other may go along with the plan but will become dependent on others to do the hard work.

Throughout the **Implementation** stage it is the responsibility of the leader to make sure that everyone does what they are meant to when they are meant to do it. This is done by outlining clear processes that align with team skills and values. Failure to do so will result in missed deadlines, conflicts and confusion.

The **Action** stage is where everything comes together. If you have paid due diligence to the prior stages, the action stage will be smooth and successful. The proper placement and synergy of your team will bring spontaneity and your targets will be surpassed time after time. Be careful not to overload your team, this may lead to success at first but will cause future burnouts.

Debriefing is essential if we are to continue being successful. Celebrating our victories and recognising what we have learnt will provide us with staying power and motivation into the next task. Debriefing also works to refine our strategies by dissecting what we have previously done in order to recognise in detail what works best and where. Recognition and praise should be plentiful at this stage as this will detour both boredom and burnout.

The seven stages naturally occur and by recognising and exploring them we are able to use these stages as signposts of our progress. Knowing the seven stages allows us to trace issues back to their source and effectively deal with them. Pay proper respect to the seven stages, they are not to be avoided.

If your team is going through a rough patch the first thing you should do is consult the seven stages and ascertain the current stage your team is in, secondly you must recognise and retrace your steps until the underlying cause is identified. As mentioned above an underlying problem will have little to do with any individual but may encompass the group as a whole.

What is Holding the Team Back and what is Pulling it Forward?

Assessing what is holding you back against what is pulling you forward is very different to creating a list of pros and cons. Pros and cons lists are costs and benefits, things which tend to be tangible. The things holding you back are usually situational variables and emotional hang-ups whilst what pulls people forward is the sense of possibility. By asking what is holding me back? What is pulling me forward? We ask ourselves positive questions which require creative answers instead of simply defining characteristics by way of pros and cons.

Do not be fearful of situational limitations, they shift constantly and in most cases are easily overcome. They should be routinely confronted.

Emotional hang-ups that come from previous bad experiences can be deep rooted and hard to spot. Properly defining your values can combat this as does taking the time out to brainstorm.

Do not make the mistake of holding any individual team member responsible for what may be holding back your team as a whole. At very worst you may view them as a symptom of the problem but never the cause. Their actions or any rebellious behaviour is, in all likelihood a reaction to legitimate issues that others have overlooked. Blame individual team members for team failings at your own peril, I'm a firm believer of the old adage "No man left behind".

Giving and Receiving Feedback

An established feedback loop acts much in the same way as rocket fuel. It propels and advances those involved beyond isolated incidents and into new territory. Feedback should not be reserved for performance based 'telling off', it is important that most of your feedback is given in the form of praise, for doing well or even not so well. When team members know their efforts are appreciate it creates an air of comradery, which is an ideal team state.

Giving feedback should be an open dialogue. Here are some tips to ensure mutually beneficial feedback.

Outline that all team members are of equal importance regardless of position or authority.

Feedback should never be accusatory, this will only serve to alienate your audience and close them off to your cause.

Asking an individual how they feel will reveal insights.

Allow people to speak for as long as they want to.

Be clear about what you want and what you need as a leader.

Be open-ended in your statements as to allow your audience to come up with solutions.

If the feedback is performance related, using language that favours your audience will be more constructive.

Avoid phrases such as "you need to" as this implies previous efforts didn't go well.

Blame does not help us move towards the future. It saps people's motivation an often leaves them feeling less resourceful. Focus on why situations arise and patterns will emerge, patterns that lead to root causes which can then be dealt with.

Keep your feedback balanced. This does not mean keeping to a set script and using it on everyone. Keeping balance often requires constant movement and readjustment in order to keep control, and it is essential to keep control when giving feedback.

Group Learning

Central to your team's potential is organisational learning which through the individuals who make up the learning process, provides results greater than its individual parts. The feedback loop created by group learning exponentially advances the learning process. If learning alone is the equivalent of learning addition and subtraction, then organisational or group learning is akin to learning multiplication and division. Or you could imagine learning alone as being on a football pitch in the dark; you are tasked with finding the ball and given a candle. Group learning instantly turns on the floodlights.

Business', organisations and teams rely on an internal flow of information and the flow of that information is dependent on how well the individuals within the team cooperate. New information and ideas are created all the time due to ever changing conditions. Make the most of this constant flow of information by getting to know your team, if possible attend a social event outside of work as a group and watch the dynamic flourish.

A simple process that can be duplicated across the organisation, developing effective training processes saves business' not only money but also provides piece of mind in that everyone is on the 'same page'.

When developing a learning process that will be used to train an entire group or organisation it is important to realise that there are many ways in which people learn. For further information into exactly how and why people process information in different ways, I suggest you look into NLP (Neuro Linguistic Programming). For now I will cover the basics of learning and learning styles. The four stages of learning are as follows:

Unconscious Incompetence

I am not aware of the action or skill.

Conscious Incompetence

I am aware of the action or skill but cannot do it yet.

Conscious Competence

I can do it if I concentrate.

Unconscious Competence

I can accomplish this task without thinking about it; the skill has now become second nature.

As human beings we possess many different ways of processing information widely referred to as the five senses. Each of us favour certain senses above others and this affects the way we learn. Here's a brief explanation of the most common learning styles.

Individuals who favour **visual** learning prefer to be shown how to complete a task or if this is not possible, visual aids such as lists, graphs and charts are a great help.

Many people favour an **auditory** style of learning where an explanation of the task and a talk through of the process used to complete it are often enough information.

A hands on or **kinesthetic** learner may find a description of the skill or task at hand hard to grasp. However showing them how the process works and walking them through the process will work wonders.

DECISION MAKING

We make hundreds of decisions on a daily basis. In modern times perhaps our decisions have lighter consequences but in the not so distant past our daily decisions were a matter of life and death. We still regularly face disruption, chaos and change and when we do we attempt understand the current events and act in a manner that is fitting. To help us understand the daily influx of information we build mental maps that structure and categorise these events in order to make them more manageable. It is these mental maps that help us to make decisions.

It is important that we are aware that our mental maps of the world are based in the way we perceive events from our individual standpoint. Therefor our mental maps are not wholly accurate, they are representations of our beliefs and past experiences that we apply to new situations in the hopes of understanding this new terrain. These mental maps do not work in every situation, it is therefore important that we are able to recognise what works where and when. Different situations have differing values, costs, benefits and risks and should be handled according to the value of the desired outcomes.

Making a good decision is not always enough; once a decision has been made it must be implemented. Implementing a decision can at times be a delicate process;

the key is to cause as little friction as possible amongst those who disagree with the decision. This is accomplished through skilful timing and consideration.

Any team should trust and respect their leader's choices; they know the decisions are strategic, not personal and that by following their leader they have the greatest chances of reaching their combined goals. The end decision will most likely be an amalgamation of the input, ideas and views of everyone in the team, breeding creativity and enthusiasm.

Decision making models are tools that help us to define the best course of action to take in any given situation. There are countless decision making models out there and I would suggest that you come up with some of your own. Before we dive into the examples I will describe the different aspects that any efficient decision making model should include.

A proper decision making model should simplify and organise current events, clarifying the costs and benefits of the courses of action available to you. Many models are visual and are very similar to algorithms and flowcharts. Finally, a decision making model does not provide the answers; it only asks questions that gather relevant information, allowing us to make fully informed decisions.

Finding Solutions

To create effective solutions you must first question your assumptions and any preconceptions you have about your abilities and what you can accomplish in the current situation.

If any limiting assumptions exist these must be dealt with before proceeding further. List your assumptions and beliefs alongside your values; those that coincide with the task at hand. Eliminate any assumptions and beliefs that do not relate to the task or are oppose to your values.

Many problems are caused by ineffective decision making and a lack of direction. Both are caused by faulty thinking and must be replaced with more efficient strategies. You cannot overcome a problem with the same level of thinking that created it.

If a business is organised and built around our market and our customers, we are in a good position to recognise what it is that is causing them difficulties. Allow customers and clients to dictate problems and issues, but never solutions. A client may be aware of an issue that's bothering them but only we are in possession of all the relevant information and so only we can make a fully informed decision. No one knows your position and situation better than you.

Successfully finding solutions and defining objectives requires that we properly access all of the opportunities, obstructions, strengths and weaknesses associated with any given issue or problem.

Once you have listed the opportunities, obstructions, strengths and weaknesses we must weigh them against each other and our values in order to discern the correct course of action.

There are five main ways in which problems can be dealt with:

Solving an issue is the easy option and is only effective in the simplest of situations. "These bags are heavy; shall we take the elevator or the stairs?" Once a situation becomes even slightly more complex 'solving the issue' is not enough.

An issue can be **resolved** by viewing the larger picture. "Out of the stairs and the elevator, which brings us out closer to our car?"

Issues and problems can instantly **dissolve** if a larger more pressing issue presents itself. "Forget the stairs and the elevator, where's the bathroom?"

Dealing with issues and problems can be **delegated** to others. "I'm staying here for a while, you go get the car and meet me outside".

By relinquishing your ownership of the problem you are **absolved**. "The heavy bags are yours not mine, stairs, elevator, it's all the same to me".

Setting Goals

When setting goals it is essential to set smaller goals along your journey, the success of each will act as a barometer or checkpoint where you can evaluate the progress and results you have achieved so far. Your overall goal as well as the smaller more manageable goals contained within should all be:

Clearly Specified/Understood

Achievable/Realistic

Measurable

Time scalable

Ethical/Positive

Relevant/Worthwhile

Safe/Legal

Interesting

Challenging

If all the above criteria are met then we are already well on the way to our established goal. The reason we set goals out in this way is that it gives us a discernible path to follow, one which can be adjusted and added to as required.

Separating feedback from criticism

Discerning feedback from criticism can be tough at times, even arduous. It is important that we put our emotions aside, especially if your project is a personal one. Before we can properly access the input of others we must first categorise the input by its level of usefulness, the categories are:

Advice "I think X needs to be changed".

Compliments "I thought it was great and wouldn't change a thing".

Criticism "It was terrible, begin again from scratch".

Team Structure Decisions

Personally I'm not a fan of rigid team structures but nevertheless they do exist and must therefore be properly addressed. Here we will look at some of the most successful team structure ideas and models currently in use. Rather than delve into explanations of the politics and psychologies behind these models I will focus only on the information and tactics that can be used today.

Empower staff and team members to make decisions, invite everyone in for the brainstorming session; they will be appreciative of the fact that their input is valued. Keep in mind that frontline staff often know more than higher management and should be involved in the decision making process.

Substitute roles and eliminate drag within a team, position your team by their individuality and personal skills. This will add an element of flow to your projects and team members will find themselves doing what they're good at; over time masters of their field will emerge.

Combine specific team members; allocate them by their skills into smaller 'mini' teams each focusing on an individual aspect of a task.

To repurpose or to put to other use is a useful strategy for keeping a team energised and up to date with their skillset. Do not delegate tasks to individuals who cannot handle them, but from time to time add to or change the role of team members to keep them on their toes.

Upgrading the skill sets of both yourself and your team is always a worthwhile endeavor.

Self-interest drives many modern workforces and target driven bonus schemes are proven to work. The drawback is that target/bonus orientated structures carry high levels of stress and burnout, little trust and a high staff turnover rate.

New Territory

When entering previously unexplored territory and situations it is important that we have the decision making skills needed to successfully avoid any unforeseen pitfalls whilst making the most of any opportunities. If we do not know which path to take we must ask ourselves the following questions in order to properly orientate ourselves and get moving in the right direction.

How did I get here/where have I come from?

To know where you are going you must first know where you came from. What events led up to this point? Will there be a change in direction here or a continuation of the current strategies and methods.

Are current events congruent with my values?

What are the five most important factors involved? Am I being motivated by negative (get away from) or positive (go towards) emotions?

Who is with me?

Whose influence can help me? Who will be affected by the outcome and in what way?

What is holding me back?

Organise all of the information you have collected so far by level of importance. From here you must discern the best course of action and set measurable goals and deadlines to help you take the first step. If there are any factors delaying your actions, list these by order of importance and make them the first goals on your list.

Whilst considering the most effective course of action consider the following:

DECISION MAKING

What do I want to do?

What is important?

What do I wish I could do?

What can I feasibly do?

What is the safest route?

What is the logical/sensible thing to do?

Which routes have I chosen in the past?

On which routes can I backtrack if any?

What is the 'norm' in this situation?

MANAGING OUTCOMES

Outcomes and Beliefs

Your outcomes are a result of your combined beliefs in **ability, possibility and worthiness** (self-worth). These beliefs must be acted upon if we wish to reach our desired outcomes. Establishing beliefs is a call to action; we naturally act upon our beliefs and so we can generally assume that beliefs that are not connected to actions are nothing but nice ideas and empty ideals.

Ability

Ability is all too often underestimated due to limiting beliefs. People regularly talk about what they cannot do; this is a dangerous habit that has the detrimental effect of limiting your learning potential. Once you have openly stated that you cannot do something your brain will believe you, and your brain does not like to be proven wrong. If you're struggling with a new skill that's ok, persevere. Only one thing is certain; *you are yet to reach the limits of your capabilities.* Always be positive about your abilities, a negative attitude and/or even basic negative talk will tie you up in a web of self-imposed limitations which will be hard to break free from. We want to be true to our word and once we openly state we cannot do something our mind will naturally close itself off to that possibility.

Remember: Stay conscious of, and break free from your self-imposed limitations.

Possibility

Many people instantly assume that something is out of the realm of possibility if they cannot see a straight line with arrows directing them to their desired goal, or if they do not currently possess the full skill-set required to complete their objective. Equally, some individuals believe things are feasible just because (metaphysically speaking) everything is possible. Do not mistake possibility with your ability. Never underestimate yourself although you should be aware of your personal limitations. You do not want to let anyone down; in the business world this is as bad as lying. The way to avoid these kinds of mistakes is to complete some basic due diligence. Do not make the mistake of thinking something is not possible due to a lack of knowledge or competence, take comfort from the fact that we do not know our true limits until we reach them.

Believing that a task is possible and that we have the ability to complete it is not quite enough. We must also have the belief that we are worthy of this task and deserve a positive outcome. Be aware of feelings of discomfort and doubt, they act as a clear sign of incongruence and must be addressed through self-development.

Cost Effective

Cost in this case is not confined to financial cost alone (see *Decision Making*).

Manage Outcomes and Obstacles

You will be confronted with numerous obstacles along your journey, many of which will be visible from a distance but sometimes you will be ambushed. When obstacles arise it's important that we correctly categorise them before coming to a decision on how best they are to be dealt with. Some obstacles will be due to current beliefs others will be legitimate real world issues. Real obstacles can be classed in one of two ways; they are either manageable and can be overturned given the time and effort. Or they are immovable objects that make achieving your goal extremely unlikely or impossible given the current timescale or circumstance. To effectively discern if an obstacle is real or a limiting belief it needs to be placed into one of the following categories:

I do not currently have the resources but they could be acquired with effort.

I have resources available to me but I am unsure what to do next.

I do not have the skills to complete this task.

The obstacle renders the outcome worthless, unethical or not worth the effort.

Once we have defined the obstacle we can then decide on which course of action we should take. The greater our attention during the categorisation stage, the more options we will have in our decision making process, which in turn increases our influence.

Directing a Conversation

Human beings, however different we like to think we are, are actually incredibly similar in practically every way. Once we realise this, we can begin to take note of the fundamental qualities and ideals that drive us all. By appealing to these fundamentals we greatly enhance our influence over a situation and our interactions will stand out above the crowd.

One of the most effective ways of directing interactions and conversations is to ask questions. Well timed questions demonstrate attention, understanding and intelligence whilst simultaneously building rapport and guiding the interaction towards your desired outcome. Making someone feel important is an ideal place to start your interaction and a great way to break the ice, start by thanking your audience for their time, accompanied by good eye contact and a warm smile.

Using open ended questions to direct a conversation takes practice, here's a few examples to get you started:

What is important to you outside of work?

How did you accomplish all that you have?

How could I gain your level of experience?

How did you feel about what happened?

What do you remember about the event?

What do you do to stay motivated?

Looking back, how would you have done things differently?

What are your suggests on possible improvements?

How could the group become more effective?

Most open questions begin with words like what, who, where and how and require more than a yes or no answer. These questions are designed to get people talking and when people are talking……we are listening, learning and gaining a greater level of understanding. Try to avoid should and would lines of questioning as these questions generally require yes or no answers.

If you're the one being questioned take your time and pause before you answer. Consider not answering the question if it will serve you better not to. Your pause will give you time to create a properly edited answer or to craft a clever dodge. **Instead of answering the question that you were asked, answer the question that you wished**

you were asked. This method works surprisingly well and demonstrates strength of character.

Conflict

There are a lot of people living in this world, all living very different lives with differing values and interests. Throughout our lifetimes we each create our own internal maps and strategies to help us survive and thrive in our in own tiny corner of the globe. No two experiences are the same; this causes each of us to develop unique strategies for dealing with the world, leading to many solutions for each problem. When a team is faced with a decision, individuals may come into conflict over which course of action to take, even though they have the same goal. Many methods will work well and complement each other, others may not. How do we settle conflicts whilst successfully achieving our goals?

There are three standard ways in which people usually deal with conflict. Flight, fight or give up are our obvious options, each with their own inherent winning or losing outcomes.

Flight

By avoiding conflict we ourselves lose and the situation may fester, there is no guarantee that avoiding a conflict will resolve the issue. We may delegate the difficult decisions to other people and they may achieve a win for our team but as individuals we will fail to gain either knowledge or experience.

Fight

Choosing to openly fight telegraphs one objective, a desire to win. For us to win, another must lose. We must be victorious. But even with our victory assured, is there a better way?

Give up

Giving up assures one thing, we gain nothing, we lose.

Compromise

A compromise is often believed to be the 'all round' best solution but in reality all parties must lose a little in order for the compromise to be met.

A True Consensus

When we reject the standard win-lose model other options begin to reveal themselves. Working in collaboration, many parties can develop new solutions preferable to a compromise.

Don't be afraid to confront issues head on even if they stir negative feelings within the group. It is always better to air and resolve any issues. Issues left unresolved fester over time and when they finally come to the forefront they will be much more difficult to deal with.

Classifying Mistakes

Mistakes come in many shapes and sizes, it is important that we classify them in order to keep everything in perspective and to learn everything we can from them. Generally speaking, people act from good intentions and mistakes are never personal. The three areas which are the cause of most mistakes are a lack of *skill*, lack of a proper *process* or a lack in *knowledge*. With these three examples as the root causes of mistakes, once a mistake is made it can usually fit into one of the following three categories:

Mind slip- When the correct process is followed but an aspect of the process is missed, incorrect or not properly completed.

General human error- When the usual process is not properly followed.

Genuine mistake- When no process or the wrong process is undertaken.

Resolution

What needs to change from here? Is it a process, training or an environmental issue?

What was the intention behind the mistake?

What have we learnt through this experience and how has it increased our understanding?

Implementing Change

Define the reasons for, and the values key to the change and list them in order of importance, this will allow you further insights into the finer details of both the required changes and the best strategies for implementing and upholding them.

How will you recognise that the change has been successfully implemented?

It is important that you write down your strategy for change, as well as the smaller goals or signs posts that will allow you to gauge your success.

When creating your strategy, pay special attention to any potential threats and develop plans for multiple possible scenarios, each assuring your success.

Request support from those around you. To fully implement a change everyone must be in agreement. Work on being able to explain the reasons for and the advantages of the change within 3 minutes. Your summary should be compelling enough to inspire your team and cement your coalition for change.

INFLUENTIAL PHRASES YOU CAN USE TODAY

There are many situations that seem daunting or awkward and so we avoid them altogether. But what can we do when we are forced to confront issues such as requesting a salary increase or saying no to a pushy individual? In this section I have laid out a number of influential phrases and strategies for getting what we want. The questions, tactics and ideas described below are designed to be used instantly and can be tried out today, go on I dare you.

Getting a Pay Rise

You deserve a pay rise, we all do. All too often people are undervalued and overworked, the problem is that most people just accept this as the status quo. Asking for a pay rise can be a nerve wracking experience but as with most things, the key is asking the right questions. The method of requesting an increase in your wage or salary detailed below is very powerful and has an extremely high success rate.

1. **Pick your battle ground**

    Don't just blurt out "I need more money!" during a team meeting. Your best bet is going to be to request to speak to your manager in private. Be sure you're asking the right person, not all superiors are able to implement a pay increase, don't waste your time, and go straight to the top.

2. **First request**

   This first request is not designed to be accepted, the first request is more of a set up for the killer question.

   QUESTION: "Thank you for your time today, I wanted to speak to you because I have a question, and you have always been very understanding towards me. Do you think you can help me? I need a pay rise............." (and then wait).

3. **Most likely reply**

   Bosses and managers routinely deal with requests for pay increases so this is nothing new to them, if they do not agree to your request it will be denied in one of the following ways:

   "We can't afford it".

   "Wait until the beginning of the new financial year".

   "We'll discuss it during your appraisal".

   "I've not got time to discuss it now".

4. **Killer blow**

   At first glance the killer blow may seem a little forward, and it is. Your superiors will not be accustomed to this style of questioning and therefor you are likely to receive an honest and positive response. Your bosses and managers are inherently good people and want to be seen as such, the killer blow will put them into a position where they are forced to view themselves in a positive or negative light.

QUESTION: "I've progressed a lot since I first started working here, what do you think I'm worth?"

At this point your boss/manager may take a second to think but the only realistic option available to them is to confirm your worth and therefor agree to a pay rise, the negotiation of amounts I will leave to you.

The above method is tried and tested which has worked time after time. It may take a little courage to ask for a pay rise but rest assured you will receive a positive outcome.

Do you think you can….?

We all need help sometimes and from time to time we may be forced to ask someone to do something that we know they rather wouldn't. Here's the best way to ask.

QUESTION: "Do you think you can….?"

This question will directly engage the person you are asking and internally they will answer yes (as long as the person has the ability and time to complete the task). Asking this question does not guarantee success, but it will give you the upper hand.

How to Say "No"

Many of us find it difficult to say "no" without feeling like we're being rude. There are many ways of saying no without actually saying "no" and here we will cover some of the most useful examples.

Counter Offer

The next time you are presented with a plan or idea you disagree with, try using the counter offer technique. The counter offer has two active parts, the agreement and the replacement. Say no to someone's idea (especially a boss) and you risk closing them off to your ideas. Instead try agreeing with the idea in principle and then suggesting either an add-on or a change in direction. For example:

"That's a great idea that would work in most cases, can I suggest…."

Outcome Comparison

What's good for the team is good for the individual, try to come up with an 'excuse' that incorporates the entire team's efforts. "I could do that, it will save time today. Or I could finish this first so we meet our weekly team target".

Ask for Advice

"Could you help me priorities my workload?"

Counter Request

"That's an idea that would work, could you help me see this idea through first?"

Loaded Questions

Loaded questions are questions that presuppose answers and are usually asked because they work in the asker's benefit. For example, if somebody seems a bit groggier than usual you might want to ask "good night last night, was it?"

Silence

Silence acts as a vacuum and when used correctly you can use it to influence countless situations. The proper use of silence is a matter of self-control; we must master staying quiet through uncomfortable silences in order to inspire both action and creativity in others. Silence is especially powerful in the field of sales when following a loaded question. Silenced matched with the correct body language can speak volumes forcing the asker to accept a 'no' before you even say a word.

Words to Start Using Today

Some words have a greater effect than others; some words instantly put smiles on our faces while others make our skin crawl.

Powerful, genius, exceptional, outstanding, energise, success, fast, desire, entrepreneurial, attract, impact, likeable, comfortable, share, appreciate, exciting, resourceful, interesting, compelling, empowering, fantastic, vivid, pragmatic, helpful, advantageous

Words and Phrases to Avoid

Lose/loser, but, fail/failure, weird, pointless, useless, boring, a little bit, just, so, bear with me, moving forward, I couldn't, I didn't want to, touching base, I didn't have much time to prepare, can't, won't, strict, rigid, maybe, attempt, try, never, catch up

Sorry

Apologising by saying sorry too often seriously impacts your influence and charisma.

Always and Never

Words like always and never, when used incorrectly can instantly close off an open dialogue and enforce self-limiting beliefs or even incite anger. No two situations are the same.

"I/They always do this" Try to think of a time when you/they did not do this.

QUICK FIRE TACTICS YOU CAN USE TODAY

A lot of skills take a great deal of time and effort to learn and use. At times all we require is a solution that works as we don't have time for an explanation of why it works. These ready to use methods will increase your understanding of your team as individuals, their feelings and the correct ways to motivate them. Below are some tips and tactics that will help you to maintain and add to your levels of influence in any given situation, clever use of these techniques will allow you greater flexibility and insight, both of which will act towards your success.

Create Tools

Creating and developing your own tools is a great way of attaining and maintaining influence over processes or behaviours. We can create models for measuring, assessing and dealing with time keeping, sales scripts, development programmes and future orientated reports to help secure our sustainability and productivity. Future orientated reports can be extremely useful tools for predicting the coming month's results. As an example of a future orientated report we could:

Review the total monthly sales for each product over the last three months. For example if we sold mobile phones, our past 3 months sales could be January=10 February=8 March= 9

Combine the totals for a chosen product for the three months. Following the above example this means we have a total of 27 mobile phone sales.

Next we divide our total sales (in this case 27) by the number of months the sales were taken over (three months). $27 \div 3 = 9$.

Our answer (9) is the average monthly sales for the past 3 months and is an accurate estimation of what we can expect mobile phone sales to be in April. This is the basis of our future orientated report.

As well as speculative sales reports future orientated reports should also consist of expected and possible unforeseen risks and opportunities. Tools and processes that entrap others should be rejected, these processes may seem full of potential but the backlash from using such unethical methods is surely not worth the possible rewards.

Become a Story Teller

When we tell a story we have the opportunity to connect directly with our listener's brains. Metaphor and suggestion are our allies and with proper use of words we are able to masterfully interact with and conduct both our team and those around us. Develop a 'set menu' or 'toolbox' of stories that will enable you to cleverly get your point across or instill in others the importance of your values. The best story tellers speak directly to the audience's subconscious, evoking powerful emotions from within our most basic motives and instincts.

Become a Translator

Superiority and authority have very little to do with knowledge and expertise. CEOs and MDs require experts to help them to properly understand patterns and results. This allows for experts to become pivotal in the decision making process. Experts use specialised skill sets to discern meaning from current events and to properly interpret outcomes and results. Translating can at times mean the ability to cleverly sum up ideas, values and obstacles in simple yet appealing ways that everyone can understand. People like people who speak to them on their level; there are many ways in which we can improve our natural ability to convey and pass on knowledge.

Pay attention to the words of others, or more correctly, pay attention to the types of words others choose to use. As previously discussed, each of us process information in slightly different ways. The best way to identify a person's processing style is by assessing their language by way of the 5 senses.

Visual thinkers use words and phrases like; see, saw, peripheral, visualise, I see what you mean, I can't see that happening, I saw that one coming, we're in the dark here, there's a light at the end of the tunnel, perspective, outlook, illustrates, well drawn out, I can picture it now.

Auditory thinkers use words and phrases like; I hear what you are saying, this opinion is echoed by the group, I like the sound of that, the tone of the message was off, sounding board.

Kinesthetic thinkers use words and phrases like; hang in there, get a grip, it is within reach, that idea gives me the creeps, stability, a weighty subject, carries momentum, cold as ice, heated debate.

Once we have noticed a cluster of these words and sayings we can adopt the same type of language for the remainder of the interaction and all following interactions. This will allow us to 'speak the same language' on an internal level leading to more meaningful connections and greater influence.

BODY LANGUAGE TIPS

Certain gestures are instantly and instinctively recognised and associated with negative feelings or discomfort. Any one of these gestures or movements alone is not enough to give definitive insights in to a person's true attitude or feelings; however a combination of these gestures, postures and movements along with the context of the situation will allow you valuable insights. You are ideally looking for a cluster of 3 to 5 body language 'tells' to begin to successfully read an individual.

Reading body language takes practice but it's a lot of fun, get into the habit of reading the body language of those around you and in no time at all you will begin to see and predict patterns and behaviours. The two main things you are looking for are signs of comfort or discomfort. With these as your starting points it will not take long to start noticing the subtleties of each, indicating to and coinciding with the emotional spectrum. Look at the below examples from the perspectives of both the speaker and the audience, then apply them to your own body language.

Frequent face touching.

Head slightly leaning to the left indicates the listener is paying close attention.

Head directed to the floor or away from the audience can mean deception or insecurity.

Lip biting or picking indicates anxiety.

Flicking of the tongue signifies discomfort.

Covering the mouth with a hand signifies discomfort or/and deception.

Low levels of eye contact can mean a number of things depending on the context, be careful not to assume someone is being deceptive as they may be self-conscious and lacking eye contact may just be a bad habit.

Excessive blinking can be caused by stress, high concentration or deception.

Gestures like hand rubbing, rubbing fingers together and fiddling with hair are known as displacement or self-comforting gestures and can indicate discomfort or boredom.

Tapping fingers or feet signifies anxiety, stress, discomfort and boredom.

Narrowing of the eyes usually indicates displeasure.

Hand rubbing usually signifies anxiety.

Crossed arms and legs indicate defensiveness or self-consciousness.

An open body language indicates truthfulness.

Both hands in view or showing palms can indicate comfort and acceptance.

Closed fists indicate anxiety, rejection, and possible frustration.

Leaning in signals the listener is paying attention.

Key emotions to watch out for are: ACCEPTANCE, REJECTION, LIKING, DISLIKING, INTEREST, BOREDOM, TRUTH and DECEPTION.

Smile

A smile conveys friendliness and confidence, there's no need to be fake, and people can naturally sense fakes and are untrusting of fake smiles. Smiling is most powerful when matched with the correct, straight, head up posture.

Smile as you enter the room.

When meeting new people (remember the eye contact).

Whilst speaking on the phone.

Throughout a presentation or speaking in public, unless context commands otherwise.

Eye Contact

Eye contact makes connections on an emotional level and can work magic for us when used correctly, but at the same time can just as easy cause us to appear as self-conscious, low value individuals. The ways in which people's eyes move can give us insights as to their current thought process. The below examples are not rules set in stone, they are general examples that alone do not carry much meaning. We must look for and notice clusters of eye movements, body language and speech patterns that all coincide with one another before we can gauge an individual's current feelings, intentions and thought processes. The descriptions below are from your (the viewer's) position, how you are looking at the other person.

Eye movement up and to the left indicates the creation of mental images.

Eye movement to the left indicates internally created sounds.

Eye movement down to the left indicates the person is experiencing feelings or bodily sensations.

Eye movement up and to the right indicates remembered pictures/images.

Eye movement to the right indicates the remembering of sounds.

Eye movement down and to the right indicates internal dialogue is occurring.

Establish Rivalries

Establishing rivalries adds to and strengthens your influence in a number of ways; it will inspire your team, breed comradery and rally supporting factors. Rivalries push us to succeed as well as demonstrating that we do not fear confrontation, this alone is enough to detour rivals and competitors.

Losers focus on the following

Who caused the event?

I am/they are incompetent.

Why does this happen to me?

I always/they always do this.

Avoid or afraid to try new things.

Problems.

BRINGING EVERYTHING TOGETHER

Whether you choose a strategic approach with long term direction, using competitive tactics and a guiding hand to optimise your team, or adopt a task focused leadership style, leading from the front and delegating to your team. You will be required to add to and adapt your current skillset on regular basis. Leaders possess extraordinary levels of commitment and dedication to self-development. Everyday should be treated as a school day and self-development, a lifelong journey.

Be non-judgmental throughout the creative processes; restrict your own judgement as well as the judgement of others until all ideas have been voiced. The brainstorming process is extremely important and should not be overlooked.

Strategic thinking skills will enhance your understanding, allowing you greater options and insights. Strategic thinkers easily anticipate change, giving them the upper hand should they act proactively.

Thinking ahead is not enough. When planning for future events or initiating change all feelings of greed/fear/self-doubt must be disregarded as they lead to emotional and unethical decisions.

Rational thinking skills will enable you to successfully understand and read others. This essential skill is the first step to influencing and leading others.

Advanced perception skills including listening skills should be practiced daily.

Rational observation (derived from knowledge and experience), and creativity are the cornerstones of influence.

Flexibility is central. Being flexible will allow you greater options and therefore greater influence.

Be clear about your goals and how they will be recognised and measured.

Always pay attention to what people are saying, how they are saying it, why they are saying it and the accompanying body language.

Develop multiple strategies for each situation in order to be prepared for any eventuality.

Look for long term fixes, short term fixes are a waste of time and effort.

Always look for the best in others.

Only be involved in worthwhile projects.

Define your values and how they relate to current events before taking action.

Beware of justifications, do the right thing.

Don't be afraid to try. When others see you putting in effort they will want to do the same.

Once mastered, your new skills will prove to be as powerful as they are valuable. You will achieve a new level of understanding, giving true ethical depth to your causes which will further rally others to help accomplish your goals.

Always be sure to act from a place of trust and cooperation unless you have opposing information. Non-cooperation should be dealt with immediately, drawing particular attention to your dissenter's lack of trust and sense of unity.

Eliminate Zero-Sum Thinking

Zero-sum thinking is an evolutionary throwback that no doubt served to protect us in the past, however now this style of thinking is outdated and even dangerous. Zero-sum thinking consists of three basic limiting beliefs:

1. **Resources are scarce, there is not enough to go around.**
2. **I must not share information and knowledge as others will use this against me.**
3. **The misfortune of others helps me. In other words, my success is added to and assured by the failure of others. Hurting others is good for me.**

The next time you catch yourself acting from any of these beliefs make a conscious effort to replace it with one or more of its respective opposite:

The available resources are greater than any individual could ever imagine let alone use.

Any resources you do not currently possess can either be created or acquired.

The open sharing of knowledge allows all parties to properly strategize, which leads to collaboration and innovation.

You could do terribly and still be doing better than your peers and competition.

AFTERWORD

Congratulations on reaching the end of **Leadership: Influential Leadership Skills for Mastering Business Communication, Management Conversations and Team Building.** This book is the first of its type, and so it is hoped that this book will enable you to break new ground with not only your own development but also with that of your team. The book was designed to enable you to create strategies that will help you to fulfil your goals and further your personal achievements. Learning to properly influence others takes time and we must first focus on ourselves, however the powerful strategies, models and influential phrases described in this book are ready to go and I suggest that you start practicing today.

The influential techniques laid out in this book are tried and tested with a few new ones thrown in for good measure, if you further develop any of the techniques we would love to hear your feedback.

ABOUT THE AUTHOR

Arthur Cannon is a well-known and respected start-up consultant and author, who has been training and coaching others across the UK since 2001. Prior to following his own path Arthur worked within sales environments as both trainer and seller for ten years whilst founding a number of start-up business' that are still in operation. Since then he has worked with many companies as a trainer and consultant as well as privately mentoring countless students in developing their own business portfolios. From his offices in Leicestershire, Arthur now operates as a start-up consultant and dedicates much of his free time to conservation projects.

www.ingramcontent.com/pod-product-compliance
Lightning Source LLC
Chambersburg PA
CBHW020444220526
45464CB00002B/846